LESSONS TILL 18

NOT A BIG LIFE, BUT A LOT OF BIG LESSONS...

SACHIN VERMA

DADAJI, ITS FOR YOU...

स्व. रामजीलाल वर्मा

01.01.1944 - 11.05.2021

Contents

Preface

I am very delighted while sharing some of my experiences through book ***'Lessons Till 18'*** *with you. This book has been written for sharing the lessons that I've learnt in these 18 years of my life.*

This book contains eighteen lessons of my life including three poems, and some other useful things. In addition to this, the book also contains Motivational Thoughts. A thorough reading of this book will help you to understand the relationship of life and problems well.

As we all know that book making is an lenghty affair. There may be some errors in the text. In this context, I request all the readers kindly make us aware about the errors and their creative suggestions are also welcome.

I hope that this book will be proven very helpful in your life.

- ***Sachin Verma***

1

The Personality Of My Grandpa

Error;
No Word Found
In My Brain & Its Around

2

The Lake Side Peace

Once, I asked a well-known writer, "Where should I go to write peacefully?" She answered that I should go to parks and sit in a corner so I could get a peaceful environment and for more peace, the lakeside area is perfect. I thanked her for her advice.

The next day, I woke up, picked up my notebook and a sparkle pen and I went to a lake nearby the city. It was so still. Only birds were there to become a part of the peace. I sat there. Soft green grass, soft breeze, waves in water, bird's mindful songs, and all the nature. I opened my notebook and took the pen. 1,2,3...10,11.....20,25....30 and so on. I spent about 40 minutes thinking about what to write about and where should I start. I didn't get any topic to write about. I picked up my notebook again and left the tiny grass which had been suffering from suffocation since I sat there. I popped out from nature's lap. All along the way, I thought about the peace that I couldn't get.

Later, one day, on a platform, I got a real peace, earlier I took that peace for granted but, with time I understood that peace is something that nature or the environment can't offer you, it is something that only your soul can offer you when there is a happiness and a good feel in our mind and soul, that is called actual peace. This is the peace that I was offered by my soul while using the buttons of the keyboard of my laptop. In that peace, instead of a heartbeat, I used to hear the click sound of the buttons, every new notification was a breath, and every word was a mine of detox. The definition of peace was changed for me. I didn't get peace while sitting near a lake but, I got the same peace while having a conversation using my wi-fi.

I get the same peace yet, and I am sure that the peace will be forever. Having this peace forever, I'll be the best of the bests. Here I am not admiring myself, just admiring my peace, my inner peace.

Ummmm......I am confused about whether I should reveal this fact or not. All right, I tell you. The fact is that all the readers of this book will read the text that I sent. Sounds weird? It's true. All those texts are so precise but, they have a different kind of meaning that only the soul can understand. Literally, the longest part of this book has been written while chatting in that peaceful environment. I am not even going to change the words to make those messages attractive, all of those selected messages have been written in the further chapters of this book. I could write those texts in a different way but, there is something called a declaration.

I have only one introverted friend, introverted for most people. I could not imagine that an introverted can take my mind out of the boundaries that used to restrict me from doing the things that I am doing right now, writing a book.

Your perspectives of seeing a peaceful place might be different. The well-known author, who advised me to try writing something while seeing a lakeside view, has a different perspective on peace and I, too, have a different one. This all taught me something, to write something or to do something like that, there is no need for thoughts but, there is a need for a soulful environment. A friend can't give us a soulful environment but, a true best friend can. Good friendship is not about being together but, it's about respecting each other's thoughts and beliefs.

Initially, this chapter was not the 2nd chapter of my book but, there is something in that 2. This will remind me of the day to thank god for making that wonderful peace that made me able to complete my book. In the future, when readers like you will read it, they will definitely understand my future vision and the simple touch of history, the history that is present today but, it will be history one day. The day will come when this book will be taken out from a bookshelf and my generations will understand these lines that seem very strange now.

Wait...I don't know what happened to me just now. I was in... where was I? What did I see?

Ohh, God! I was in a dream of future, this is my problem, I lose my topic just because of my emotional intellectuals. Sorry, if you couldn't understand the above paragraph. Writing this chapter, I am taking a decision that this chapter of my book, not only this but, no chapter of my book will be sent to the editor to decorate the language with words because the editor can only edit my words to make the book more standard. I don't like that because the editor can't write my feelings in his words and decorated language. This isn't a book, it is just a promise that I made. I have not been writing anything for a long time but, a day ago I got the reason to make the book ready to publish. I know that whatever I have written about my soulful and mindful peace is not sufficient but, it's alright. The intro of intro should not go longer.

3

Cry to Beep

Remembering the day
When I cried
Holding my hand
Mom standing aside.
I was introduced to the class
Well, my first day it was.

Cry, cry, cry till the bell rung
Not a single friend all of the among.
As bell rung, all started to run,
Taking out by a teacher, wasn't a fun.
With my tears, I went in the lap,
My beloved place to take the nap.

The homework diary became a part of routine,
The routine was there till thirteen.
The level of excitement
Never came again.
No more pencil,
I got a pen.

With every new session,
Lost some friends.
What about my gang?
It always extends.

The best of memories in the corridore,
Why till 12th? The school should be more.

The first bravery, to bunk the prayer,
In the store room, my gang was there.
Everytime we worried about being caught,
But, everyone was a player not a bot.
No fear of punishment untill we were together.
Could I enjoy the bunk alone? Never.

Played holi at the water cooler,
Got complained by a chap.
The cruel iron ruler,
The musical slap.
On friend's turn, my toungue was flexed.
Feet got colder knowing I was the next.

Later, started to be called senior,
We considered ourselves as the superior.
It was the time
When friends were a family,
It was my gang,
Made me able to speak cammily.

With a wink, It was a farewell.
Smiles were on faces, but hearts weren't well.
We were dancing, things were so fast.
Wanted to cry, knowing it was the last
Chance, to make promise to friends
To be forever,
In that farewell, Not only friends
The whole class was together.

We wanted to cry like the day first,
But, suppressing our emotions, We just wept.

4

The Colour of Dark

I wrote this poem while thinking about the pain and problems that blind people have to face daily, every hour, every single minute.........every second, they face something hard that normal people can't manage. I know it's impossible to feel the actual pain that they face but, I just wrote whatever I could imagine.

Not able to see
The beauty and its flash.
Do they care or ask me
To scratch my gash?

How beautiful is this world?
Want to examine all I heard.
The day is bright,
The night is dark.
Meaningless for one
Who hasn't seen a spark.

Without any vision,
I have a view.
Feels the same
In every new
Morning, that begins
When I want.

Willed to break me
but, it can't.

Do colors exist?
Not for me.
I would choose my favourite,
If I could see.

Brings stress,
The social isolation.
I'm given a place to sit,
On every family occasion.

Wish to get around
The city and luxury.
But, stepping out on the ground
Require a hard memory.

Making me, did God hasten?
Or as a gift, it was graven
In the lines on my palm.
Sometimes it hurts but, I'm calm.

On the contrary, finds my Goodluck.
Accepts my reality, having no truck.
Also, I'm able to find the beauty
Not the face, but the heart is pretty.

If I were blind,
The poem would be long.
But can't write more,
My imagination isn't so strong.

It is the second poem that I've written in my life till now. One more thing is here that I would like to share with you, I wrote this poem when the editing work of this book was being done. The editor advised me to make the poetry section of the book the last of the book, but I believe that this poem holds that beauty to be the face of this entire book. I'm not talking about the beauty of literature because I haven't learned the "L" of literature so how could I talk about literature? I am talking about the beauty of my creation as compared to my other creations. Let it go.

I don't want to be shared,
I love to live paired.
Having a company
Of You,
No one else, in this world.

My imagination
To attain the ben.
We'll live together
After crossing the lion's den.

Crossed the limits,
A few left.
It's my heart,
Where you're kept.

Remembering the date
When we met,
I sit in moon light
Till late.

The wind comes
To murmur in my ear.
Losing you,
Is my only fear.

I got the words
You sent.
Trying to understand
What it meant.

Love for you
Will not end
Like the ink of pen
In my hand.

6

A Cheating

What do you think about cheating in classes, exams, etc? We are always advised to not cheat anyone. But in my case, cheating became my life changer and also a class changer which made me different from others, even in my class, it made me different. In 2019, I had only one weak point in my life, which was 'English'. Yes, English! The language that I am writing today. I know that my level hasn't become so good, but for me, it was an unexpected thing in 2019. On 7th July 2019, I was in the classroom, suddenly a man entered the classroom and introduced himself in English. If I lie, I understood everything that he said. Then he started saying something in English, very fluently. For the next 40 minutes, he just spoke. Till now I don't know what did he say that day, but I liked it. After finishing the lecture, he wrote a word on the blackboard, the word was 'Present'. He asked me to read that loudly, but I couldn't read that word properly. All the students got a hidden smile on their faces. That day, I decided to learn English like him and I was very strong-willed about that. But there were a lot of hurdles in my way. First was my fear, which was restricting me from studying, whenever Mr. Puneet asked me to speak in the class, My tongue got paralyzed because thinking had been developed in my mind that whatever I speak would be wrong.

One day, Mr. Madan gave us homework to translate the story of thirsty crow into English. I didn't want to be a reason for laughing for other students again. I wanted to do something and I did. I took help from google and translated the story into English. I was very excited to speak out about that story in the class because I knew that that day everything was going to happen well. I was very confident in the translation that I did.

In the classroom, Mr. Puneet gave chance to all students to speak their translations. My chance came, I spoke my translation very fluently, because of confidence. For the first time in my life, Puneet sir clapped for me and he told the entire class to clap for me. I was stunned.

I didn't know that those claps would change my life. That was the day when the actual confidence came to me. I became really motivated. From that day, I started my journey as an English learner. The thing that is taught in class primary and middle classes, I learnt in my high school, and today, when I am writing this all on a paper, I am really glad. It may be a silly thing for you to write or speak in any language, but for me, it was a terror. Now it is my pleasure. Who can think that cheating can change someone's life? That cheating changed mine.

I am not promoting you to cheat someone or cheat in exams. I just shared this incident because I learnt an important lesson from this incident. Everyone has mines of confidence inside them, but the only thing that is needed is a worker who can bring out the confidence from the dark mines. The worker may be your teacher, friend, family member, relative, close person, etc. One more worker is there, You. When the confidence inside you is brought out by someone else, it may no longer be very soon. When you bring out your confidence by yourself, it never ends, never.

Confidence can make you faster than problems, bigger than hurdles, stronger than dilemmas, and better than you too. You can trust these words because a boy who couldn't speak or write due to a fear of being a joke, is writing a book that is going to be published. I know that I've done a lot of mistakes in this book. I know that I will be judged by my readers on the basis of my mistakes. Still, my confidence is giving me the enthusiasm to let this book be published.

7

Are you the best?

Once, I was challenged to be the best in my class. I took it so seriously and I started copying the toppers of my class. I copied their study method, routine, way of speaking, body language, way of writing, etc. I was an average student in my class, but as I started copying the toppers, I lost my naturality and after some time I became the dumbest student in the class. Everything was ended for me. I lost myself, I lost my version, and I lost the respect that I was given when I was a good student. When I remember this phase of my life, a line comes to my mind, "In search of gold, we lost diamonds." Trying to be the best, I became the dumbest.

While writing this book, I am thinking what is the actual meaning of being best? Best in a friends group or best in a class or best in a school or best in a city or best in a state or best in a country or best in the world. None of these, I think. It took several years for me to understand the actual meaning of being the best.

What is the actual meaning of being the best? Being the best is not a comparative case, we don't need to compare ourselves with others in the case of being the best. Being the best stands for being the best version of ourselves. First of all, we have to find the limitations of our performance and efficiency then we should go towards the second step. The second step is to come out of our comfort zones where we make ourselves bound. Once we come out of our comfort zones, then only the changes will come to make us the best version of ourselves, and that's all, being the best stands for.

I had lost my version because I didn't know what the word 'best' stood for. I had lost my dreams when I lost myself for being the best. Thanks to God for sending Vivek Sir and Puneet Sir into my life, they rebuilt my own version, and I got my naturality back. They are not just teachers for me, they both are my second parents. Lots of teachers came into my life and they all have a special space in my heart, but Puneet sir and Vivek sir are different from the others. For me, they are founders of myself. I was given my dreams back by both of them. They are.......I have no more words to explain them.

Ohh...sorry! I lost the point that we are talking about.

The word 'best' also has lots of negative aspects. When we are compared with someone who is better than us, we consider them the best and consider ourselves dumb and looser. That put our confidence in the volcano of never-ending frustrations. We should compare ourselves with ourselves only. We should just try to be better than the older version of ourselves, only ourselves. If there is a need, one should not be ashamed to ask for help, I've also asked for help from my friends to review my book and to give suggestions to me for making this book best, best means better than what I am writing.

I have one more story of my life which relates to this book, actually, it is the reason why I am writing this book? My first book was published in 2019 named 'The Painter'. I haven't given that book to Puneet sir yet, because, I wanted to show him the best book written by me, but here 'best' doesn't stand for the best of all time, 'the best' stands for the best book written by me. I know that this book 'Lessons till 18' is going to be better than my previous book 'The Painter' so, I can say that this book is my best book. That's all I know about being the best.

Most people try to become the best they try to pass every test, and they try to be successful in their life, but they can't achieve their aims. Where the mistake is? The mistake is that they always tried to become better than others, better than their ideals. All the successful persons say that they had just tried to be better than themselves only. They only tried to expand their abilities and capacities. It's a good thing that we follow others who are successful, It gives us the motivation to be something like that, but one should understand the major difference between following someone and trying to be like someone. Following someone leads us to learn new things from the actions and mistakes of successful personalities, whereas trying to be like someone makes us placed in confused and confused only because God makes us be ourselves not someone else. Trying to be like someone else is just a way to insult God's decision as he made us the unique version of ourselves. Don't try to be like someone else, Let others try to be like you.

8

In a fix

One day, when I was in a classroom and my teacher Mr. Puneet Madan was teaching writing skills. Suddenly, he asked all the students to gather around his desk and he borrowed 10 pens from me. We all gathered around his desk, Mr. Puneet made a pattern on his desk using those 10 pens, and meanwhile, he gave us an instruction to focus on his body gesture along with the pattern. He took 2 minutes to complete his pattern and after making a random pattern on his desk, he asked us to find out a digit that was hidden in that pattern. I was very confident that I could find the digit in that pattern. I observed that pattern from every angle and I tried my best to find out the digit, but I couldn't. A girl named Shilpa, who was standing beside me answered, "three".I was amazed because that was a meaningless pattern and that girl found a digit in that. I was flummoxed.

After admiring the girl, Mr. Puneet picked a pen from that pattern and placed the pen on the upper side of the pattern. He again asked us to find a digit in the pattern. As he asked, the girl answered, "Sir, it is 4". Now I started becoming completely puzzled.

It didn't stop there, Mr. Puneet again picked a pen from that pattern and placed it at another corner of the pattern. This time, the same girl answered before the teacher could ask. I was frustrated and I could say nothing. The girl made me speechless.

Your listening skills and focus are amazing, the teacher said. After admiring the girl, Mr. Puneet came towards the secret trick that he used while asking the question. He said, "The pattern is nothing, it doesn't mean anything." We all keep silent, he continued, "This is just a random arrangement of pens, I also don't know which digit is hidden in it." We laughed, Mr. Puneet said, "You all got stuck in the problem, you were completely focused on the problem, except Shilpa. Now recall the instructions that I gave you before making this pattern. I asked to focus on my body gesture and the pattern as well, but you all kept your complete focus on the problem only. That's why you couldn't find the solution." Where the solution was? We all asked. "The solution was on the edge of the table, actually I was indicating the answers by my fingers at the edge of a table, that's why I told you to focus on my body gesture too." This made us amazed, totally amazed.

The teacher continued, "The same thing happens in our life when problems come in our way, we only keep our eyes and concentration only on the problems and due to this, we take a long time to overcome the problems, and meanwhile we are exhausted by the problems. The solutions stay nearby the problems, but it is required to change our point of view and way of thinking to see those solutions which always hide around the troubles."

The most amazing lesson that I learned from this game of pens was 'Don't be exhausted by your problems, let's exhaust the problems. Focus on the way to solutions instead of focusing on the problems.'

It is extremely easy to say to focus on the way to a solution, but in reality, it is much harder to understand the difference between focusing on the problems and dealing with the problems. These two things possess a great contrast with each other. Focusing on the trouble causes a bad effect on our minds, but dealing is another way to overcome the waves of trouble while going forward in our life without any hurdles. Troubles are just like thunderous waves in which we can't swim on the surface, if one wants to be safe from horrifying waves the one must go down in the waves holding a long breath. Many people lose their lives in the strong waves of the ocean because when the waves come, they try to stay on the surface of the water which becomes the reason for their death. And one who knows about the technique of being safe in the waves goes down in the water, where the velocity of water is less than the velocity of water on the surface.

The same thing happens in our life we see the problems with a wrong vision and we got stuck. but, one who has a different point of view sees the problems correctly, and as a result, problems are solved.

There is a way to know the way to solutions of troubles, which is, by observing the thing which is going on around us. I am not saying to observe an attractive person, which mostly happens with the teenager. Observing means, learning new lessons from the small things going around us, like I learned a big lesson from a game of pens. In the same way, you have millions of chances to learn about the truth and reality of life.

One more question arises here. What to do when problems are beyond our control? It happens, that sometimes the problems seem very hard to be solved, and we become helpless in these types of conditions. My personal favorite way to resolve these conditions is...Let the things happen and smile. Sounds weird? I know, it is the hardest thing to do. But,...wait, wait, wait. Before writing about this, I would like to share a story with you.

Once, a group of the saint was doing some 'sadhana' in a monastery. Those were extremely hot days, a young monk wanted to drink lime juice, he made a glass of lime juice but unfortunately, he added much more lime juice to the water. The taste of the juice was no longer good. This was a problem beyond the control of the monk. He couldn't remove the lime juice from the water. He had two ways before him. The first was, to make a new glass of lime juice and waste that one. The second was, to share the problem with others to change it into pleasure. He chose the second one. He added 3 more glasses of water and the juice became so tasty. He shared the juice with his colleagues and they all had the good pleasure of drinking a cold and sweet drink on the days of hot summer.

I think you have understood what I am going to write further. The monk didn't focus on the problem, he dealt with that. And that's why he made everything good. He changed the problem into a moment of happiness with his colleagues.

9

An Ignored Cold Morning

It was an extremely cold Friday morning in December 2021, I was going to my friend's house for revising the concepts for the exam. Two hours were left for the exam. I wore a t-shirt, a shirt, and a jacket too. Still, my teeth were showing their anger by producing a sound like a woodpecker's work. Walking on the street, I saw something unusual. A boy of about 4-6 years, naked... completely naked. He was playing with garbage there. It seemed like the boy was ignoring the cold morning. I was in hurry, I ignored him and went to Jatin's house.

I couldn't focus on my study at Jatin's house. When we left Jatin's house, I shared that scene with Sourabh, Jatin, Nitin, Gopal, and Manish. We all decided to meet the next day. It was Saturday, We met and took a decision that we would collect the old clothes from our houses and make them ready to wear. The next day, Sunday, We had collected clothes for all age groups, we had mostly woolen clothes that were a good thing for those cold days. All those clothes were collected from our houses and apartments only.

Manish, Gopal, Nitin, Jatin, Sourabh, and I went to the same area where I had seen that naked boy that morning. We found him there, he was playing there naked with some other children. Most of them were naked. They all were showing their power to the coldness of that morning. We called them and distributed the clothes among them. One of us had captured this on his mobile's camera. We decided to upload that video on our Facebook page named 'We With Them' that we had created. Just a day after uploading that video, we received a lot of good comments and messages from our viewers. Those messages and comments gave us a boost and enthusiasm to do more work like that.

Not everything went well. One of my relatives made a call to my parents and said, "Do you know what is sachin doing?" Yes, we know, my parents replied very confidently. My relative continued, "He should not upload all these videos on social networks because in these videos it can be seen that he is throwing garbage from his houses, they are distributing old clothes. Old clothes are not a big issue, but videos should not be uploaded if they are sharing old things." My parents gave an amazing reply, "We are with our child because he is eligible to take decisions for himself, whatever he is doing, we are with him... You don't need to take any stress about him and his work." My dad told me about it the next day. I thought about it and decided that I would not do this again and I would also delete the videos from the Facebook page.

I shared this with my friends also, they all were demotivated like me. They all decided the same thing that I had decided. 'We With Them' was going to be ended.

The same day, we were going through the same way, on which I saw the child for the first time that morning. This time, the scene was different. The children were playing in the same roadside area, but this time, they had covered their bodies with the clothes, that we gave him. For them, their looks were no less than a Hero's look. When we had seen them last time, they had no cloth on their body, but this time they had something on their body. After seeing that, we all became energetic. It was enough for us to get our motivation back to do our work continuously. We kept our work continue.

Whenever we shared a video, we got a lot of good messages that motivated us every time. After some time, the group of 6 friends had been turned into a group of youth. Lots of people joined us through Facebook and Instagram. We received lots of support from different cities in India. Not even India, for starting a free educational website, we received help from Australia too. These things took us on seven clouds.

We will keep our work continuing...forever.

Many people think to do some work for public welfare, they wish to do so, and just wish to do so. They never start. Why? because they only want to do something big. Do big things start from big? Not at all. If you want to climb a mountain, you have to start downhill. No one can achieve the top without going through the way which starts from the down. Things are started from zero and with hard work and consistency they are brought to the top.

Remember this thing in every phase of your life. Whenever we start something with zero, we may not have a good response and a big team, but our work brings love to you. In the same way, our videos bring love from our viewers and supporters.

Hurdles are the parts of a way to success. Hurdles come to test our will. We may lose our confidence and motivation facing these hurdles, but after every high wave of demotivation, there is a next wave that comes with lots of new energies and motivations.

10

Dustbin of Past

The dustbin is a large container for rubbish that you keep outside your house. Is the dustbin only a box in which we can throw the garbage? For me, the dustbin has a different meaning in my life, the dustbin of my life allows me to throw unwanted thoughts into it.

Happening bad and unwanted things to us is normal. It happens to us all, but most people become monotonous due to those bad memories of their lives that happened in past. They just spend a big portion of their lives thinking about the past because they don't have any dustbin in which they can throw their bad past memories. A few have that dustbin in which they can throw their bad memories of the past. The bad memories of the past make us slower, sometimes they make us stop in the present due to which one can't live in the present. In fact, the regretful remembrances of the past have the power to regulate what we do in present.

This dustbin of the past is not bought from any market. It can be bought from our willpower, the willpower to be the best variant of ourselves, the willpower to get the most excellent output from ourselves. This dustbin is just a decision that only a strong-willed person can take. The decision is that I will establish a dustbin in my mind and throw all the negative aspects of the past into it. This dustbin should have a perfect cap so that the thing that is thrown once can't be picked out again. If your willpower is not at the highest level that one can have, then the dustbin can be faded anytime when it is filled completely and all the garbage of past memories will be spread on the floor of your present. Trust me, this will ruin your present and future as well.

If we want to live a life we should have a bright personality and future, then we have to escape the prison of past memories. The bad memories of the past build a prison in our minds if we don't let them go. The negative remembrance of the past does not stay in our minds, we keep it. Yeah! we keep it in the house of our present life where they build their empire quickly. In this empire, there is only one room for our present and future, actually, that room is a prison where our present and future are kept and tied by the rope of frustration.

I know a great formula to focus on the present, to focus on what we are living today. "Let it go," It is the best way ever to be free from the prison of our past memories. Whenever any unwanted thing happens to us, it gives us an internal despondency in our minds and soul. After having any unwanted thing, we should let it go because, we can't change the past by worrying about it, so let it go. Don't let everything go that happened in the past, but the things that can't be changed and corrected should be sent away from the flame of our minds. If there is any chance to change that thing, then we should change it, if it can give a moment of joy to anyone you love or like.

One more thing that we should keep in our mind is that we should only forget the bad part of our past not what it taught us. Our bad past can be the best teacher for our better future, our good past makes us happy and our bad past makes us strong and brave to face the same condition again in our life, the condition that broke us in our past. Putting our bad past into that dustbin of past, we should pick out the lessons from that piece of the wicked phase of our life. Past teaches a lot to an individual.

Mistakes allow us to create an unhappy past, an unhappy past allows us to learn new things, and learning new things allows us to be prepared for the same mistake in our future, this makes us perfect. Don't worry about mistakes, think about the ways you can correct them. Then we get a forward vision in our present for a happy future.

I remember a story that taught me about the dustbin of the past. The story was....hmm..... sorry! My dustbin of past has a thick and strong cap over it, I can't look inside it. So sorry:)

11

The Longest Chapter

I thought you're mine.
One who reminds me that
Things will be fine.

12

A joyful demotion

Back in 1999, there was an adult boy, he had the responsibilities of his mother and a physically challenged younger brother. He started working in a cloth store. He was given 1000 rupees as a monthly salary. Working in that shop, he kept his study continue. He worked hard, but there were lots of hurdles in his way. At that time, he didn't know that he had a bright future ahead. He believed that his whole life would be the same as it was.

One day, an old lady, lived near the house of that boy. The old lady called the boy and said, "I am no more a teacher. I left my job as a teacher in the school. Now I want to have rest." You should take some rest, the boy replied. The old lady said, "I called you here because I know that you can be a good teacher, You can join the school at my place. Will you?" Yes ma'am, I will, the boy replied. The only lady continued, "Alright, I will talk to the principal and you go to school and meet him." Alright Ma'am, Thanks! Thank you so much!

The boy went to school and met the principal, after getting the reference of that old lady, the principal hired the boy as a primary teacher in his school. For this job, the boy was going to be paid 600 rupees as a monthly salary. After knowing about the salary, the boy was flummoxed because the salary was nearly half the salary that he was paid as a salesboy in that store. He decided to teach there for a few days and then decide what to do.

The next day, He reached the school on time. Prayer was done by the students, classes were started. The boy was said to go to the primary classes only. He entered a primary class, and all the children sitting there stood up and said, "Gooood mooorniinggg teeaacchhheeer." For the first time, the boy was given that much respect. He was called "Sir." For the first time, it was happening. He was on the seventh cloud. He decided to continue that job and leave the job as a salesman. He knew that he will be given nearly half the salary than the last job, but he was delighted to receive that respect.

For the first time in his life, the boy enjoyed a job. He was very strong-willed to make his career in the field of education. After the hard work of years, he achieved his dreams and became a government teacher. Now, he doesn't only teach the students a subject, he teaches his students everything that a student of a big school knows. He has been changing the lives of his students. The students of the govt. school, in which he teaches, can speak English more than the students of a big school. He is getting lots of good wishes for his work.

Do you know who is that boy? The name of that boy is Puneet Madan, my teacher.

This story of his life teaches me about the difference between 'doing a job' and 'enjoying a job.' This may seem to be a silly thing, but this is the thing that differs between a life and a happy life. When Punit sir worked in a shop, he was paid more, he had been doing that job. When he joined the school and started teaching, he was paid less, but he enjoyed the job. When our work becomes our passion then we get actual success. We can't neglect this fact.

Do you know what is the relation between the clock and success? I, too, don't know more about it, but a little bit, I know. When we do our work according to the clock, we may earn money and fame. When we do our work ignoring the clock, we never get frustrated and tired with our work. Only a few people have this ability to work ignoring the clock and these few people are those, whom we consider our ideals. These people live on the top, the top of success. I am not saying to ignore a timetable, I am saying to expand our abilities and get out of our comfort zone. The Comfort zone doesn't let us win, it makes us lazy and a person with limited abilities. Let's be expandable.

13

The Teacher Mother

This chapter of my book is very close to me, it relates to my life. I'll describe it at the end of the chapter. Also, there is a wonderful fact about nature.

There is no school in this world where baby giraffes go for learning about life and its requirements. But they learn a very important lesson rather early in life. How early? Just after a few minutes of birth. This lesson is taught by the mother giraffe. We learn a lot about our life and pains.

The birth of a baby giraffe is the very and first painful thing for the baby giraffe as well as the mother giraffe. The baby falls from a height of about eight feet from the ground. The weak baby falls very badly.

Initially, the mother giraffe lovingly lowers her neck and smooches the baby giraffe. Then secondly, a very horrifying and incredible thing happens. She lifts her long leg and kicks the baby giraffe with the complete power that she has. It sends the baby giraffe on a small air journey, baby falls to the ground. As the baby falls to the ground, the mother kicks the baby again, again, again. And again. Until the baby giraffe learns to stand on its feet and run.

Happy to see the baby giraffe standing on its own feet and looking around, the mother giraffe comes to the baby giraffe and gives another kick. This time, the baby giraffe falls, but stands very quickly and recovers from the pain so fast. Mother Giraffe is delighted because she knows that the baby giraffe has learned to stand up after falling down. She knows that baby has learned that: Never mind how hard you fall, always remember to pick yourself up and get back on your feet.

The mother giraffe does this due to her chief concern, to save her baby from the lions and leopards. Lions and leopards love giraffe meat, especially baby giraffe meat. Very first, the mother teaches to stand up, then to run, then to recover quickly. These lessons are the only weapons that the baby giraffe has to be safe from lions and leopards.

Most of us are not so lucky as baby giraffes. Most of us are not taught to stand up every time we fall. Most of us are not taught to stand up after falling down, grow again when we are down, and restart things when we give up. No one kicks us to bring us out of our comfort zone, no one teaches us to bounce back.

But, a few lucky people get someone in their lives who teaches us these all things in their lives. If you study the life of successful people. Were they always successful in all works that they did? Not at all. Did success come to them very easily and quickly? Not at all. They just had lots of ups and downs, falls, failures, bounce backs, and re-startings.

In my own life too. I fall lots of time, but I have been taught to stand up again and again. After every failure, I stand again. I'm not saying that I'm successful in my life. Not at all, but somewhere I am successful. I have successfully got control of my emotions, my feelings, and my mood. I could do this all because whenever I fall, I stood up and tried to learn from my mistakes and improve them. That is enough for having a smile on my face

14

Missed Dronacharya

Dear reader! How've you been?

Before considering the topic that I am gonna discuss in this chapter of my book, I would like to ask you something. Tell me, Why should you read this chapter? Why should you pay attention to my thoughts?

Considering the same thoughts, I saved an amount accumulated by my father's hard-working. I saved almost 6 lakhs just in a moment. Are you fond of knowing it?

As soon as I Passed class 10th, my father asked me to go to Kota for my JEE preparation. My all friends were about to go to Kota but, I denied my father. I didn't go there to be trapped. Actually, there is a big reason beyond it. I'll tell you about it in our further discussion.

What are the concepts in your intellectual to differentiate a teacher and a businessman? In my view, one whose passion is teaching is a teacher and one whose profession is teaching is a businessman. Teaching has never been a profession. In today's era, mostly there are businessmen in the education field. Education has become the fastest-growing business. As a student struck in class 11th, the actual business starts there. Lots of businessmen from various fields come to that student and try to attract the student towards the field where they work, where they can make the student a profitable customer. They don't care about the actual field of interest of a student, they wash the brain and set up a trap to catch those students. A teacher who teaches for JEE or NEET, advises opting for science in Higher Secondary. A teacher who teaches accounts advises opting for Commerce. The same thing is being done in every stream.

Students do not opt for their field of education, they are made to opt for their field of education according to the desire of a guide. I am not saying that every teacher is doing the same, but most of them do.

There is a need for teachers like Dronacharya, the guru of Pandavas. He knew that teaching them all different kinds of skills would be difficult. He could teach them all a single skill and they all would master that skill too but, Dronacharya was a real teacher who teach with passion. He observed their field of interest, then he decided to teach them skills according to their capabilities.

In the present era, no one cares about the capabilities and field of interest of the students. The teachers who teach professionally, are making success harder to achieve. If we go to Kota and try to see the top of the buildings of some coaching institutes, we may fall. It seems that lord Kuber lives in those buildings and pours golden sand from heaven's break over those institutes.

Just like other writers, I, too, can write so many things about the education system of India. I don't only write about it, I work to bring a change. That's why I am gonna start CLASSMATE TEACHERS (**www.classmateteachers.com**) which will be a place where students will be guided in a perfect manner. My lifetime rule for this company is "Nothing will be charged from students as any service charge."

Most of the students are misguided and they are forced to climb the tree even if they are masters in swimming. Getting my point? According to a survey, 80% of students in India don't even know what are those fields of working that they can opt-in in order to achieve their dreams. They are shown only some most prestigious institutes, they are forced to have a tag of those institutes. There are lots of ways, to get everything in life, but the need is, to make the students aware of choosing their future. Our TEAM DRONACHARYA does the same work, this team has different representatives who are veterans of mentorship. For each and every student in this world, the personal guidance of this team is free....forever...

We are very strong willed to make free courses for the students to have some more extraordinary learning.

15

Correctly Wrong Timing

Wrong Timings,
Sometimes make
Right coincidences.

16
A World in the World

Writing,
The best way to make a world in this world
Which is much bigger than the actual world.

17

The Boarder Line

It was the evening of the 14th of November, 2021. I was so excited and enthusiastic. Why? After a few hours, I was going to be 18. It is a great feeling when we are no more a child, according to us. My friend sent me a quote that gave me an idea to write about this topic. It was something about the legal privilege that a child gets at the age of 18. Which type of privileges? To opt for whatever we want? To go wherever we want? To stay out of home? To decide about us ourselves?

Is this freedom? I don't think so. This is a separation from our actual and merry life. 18 is not a time when we should be independent, it's a time not to stay totally dependent. Being 18 is not excitement, waiting for being 18 is an excitement. Being eighteen means we are able to manage most of the problems by ourselves. This is the age when our mind diverts in wrong ways where we would find nothing at all, except the separation that I mentioned in the first line of this paragraph. 18 is the age when we may look physically strong but, it's also an age of having lots of mental pressures that cause mental weakness.

Nothing was changed turning 18 but, everything was changed trying to understand why was nothing changed turning 18? I have been so eager to have new experiences frequently. So, One day, I just lay on the bed, turned the light off, and started to create some scenarios in my mind. What about its effect on me? Every night before going to bed, my mind started to get upset. Don't know why? Not only this, but sometimes I cried. This is the complication of being 18 years old. Without any reason, the mind develops stories, dreams, scenes, demands, feelings, and lots of complications.

In my view, it is the toughest time for an adult child to manage the mental pressure of expectations that our parents, relatives, and friends have.

Friends may create mental pressure but, soulmates always make us free. In my case, I never took mental pressure because I had lots of soulmates and some of them are really awesome, and what about that memer friend? Breathtaking.

In the case of expectations of family, I am lucky. I know that my family, too, has a lot of expectations from me for sure but, they never let me know that they expect anything from me, anything at all. Dreams are obvious, their dreams are to see my dreams coming true. Whatever I decide to do with my life, they support me. Before 18 and after 18 as well.

For most students, it is the time to opt for the best way to reach their designation. Usually, students complete their schooling at 17-18. In the last year of schooling, we get an incredible level of excitement to enjoy life after school life. Is there anything special after the 12th that school life doesn't offer us? Yes, comparatively more responsibilities, more options to make us confused and career-related decisions. I don't think that after 18 life is better than the life before 18. In case you really want to see glimpses of happy moments of school life have a look at chapter 3 of the book.

We get lots of opportunities to discover the dark side of everything. As a child, we see the brighter side of the world but, as an adult, we realize that the side we have been seeing is just a myth, an actual reality far from these myths. There is one more truth, In case we want to have a happy life, explore the dark side, and have known all the aspects come back to the bright one for the rest of our life.

That feeling that we are now 18 + is amazing, a feeling that we can conquer the world, and all of a sudden a thought comes to mind to choose a career option. We get a new college to have to change for higher studies and explore the hostel life. Remember that, freedom always comes along with lots of responsibilities. Most of the school friends leave because they go to other cities for their studies and we, too, go somewhere for making our career. We understand that everything in this world is actually connected with money, except a few. One who can manage his mind at the age of 18, would definitely achieve the ben. It's a universal truth.

18

Just A Random Note

My last note was written something about 10 days ago and since then I had not written anything because I only write when there is a reason. I had lots of reasons when I started to write this book. During the journey of writing this book, I lost my reasons or motives a lot of times. We can easily understand it, if I am writing it then definitely I have a reason to do so. A reason to finish my work as soon as possible is just to have a feel of enjoying a glimpse of heaven's happiness.

In my view, sometimes we are not able to do most of the things, situations make us unable to take a suitable and future decorator decision. There is only a single way to do those things. Having a reason or motive to do something in life, a normal person can do abnormal things. Most people think that whatever they have achieved in their lives is just because of their hard work only. My views are different. Success depends on hard work but, to do that hard work we need a motive.

Declaration

I, the author, will write the second part of this book whether the first part "Lessons Till 18" receives a good response or not. I know that this isn't a south movie that you'll wait for. I don't care about the sales and response of readers, I love to read my creations later. That's what I write for.

Printed by Libri Plureos GmbH in Hamburg,
Germany